THE SPECTATOR
CARTOON BOOK

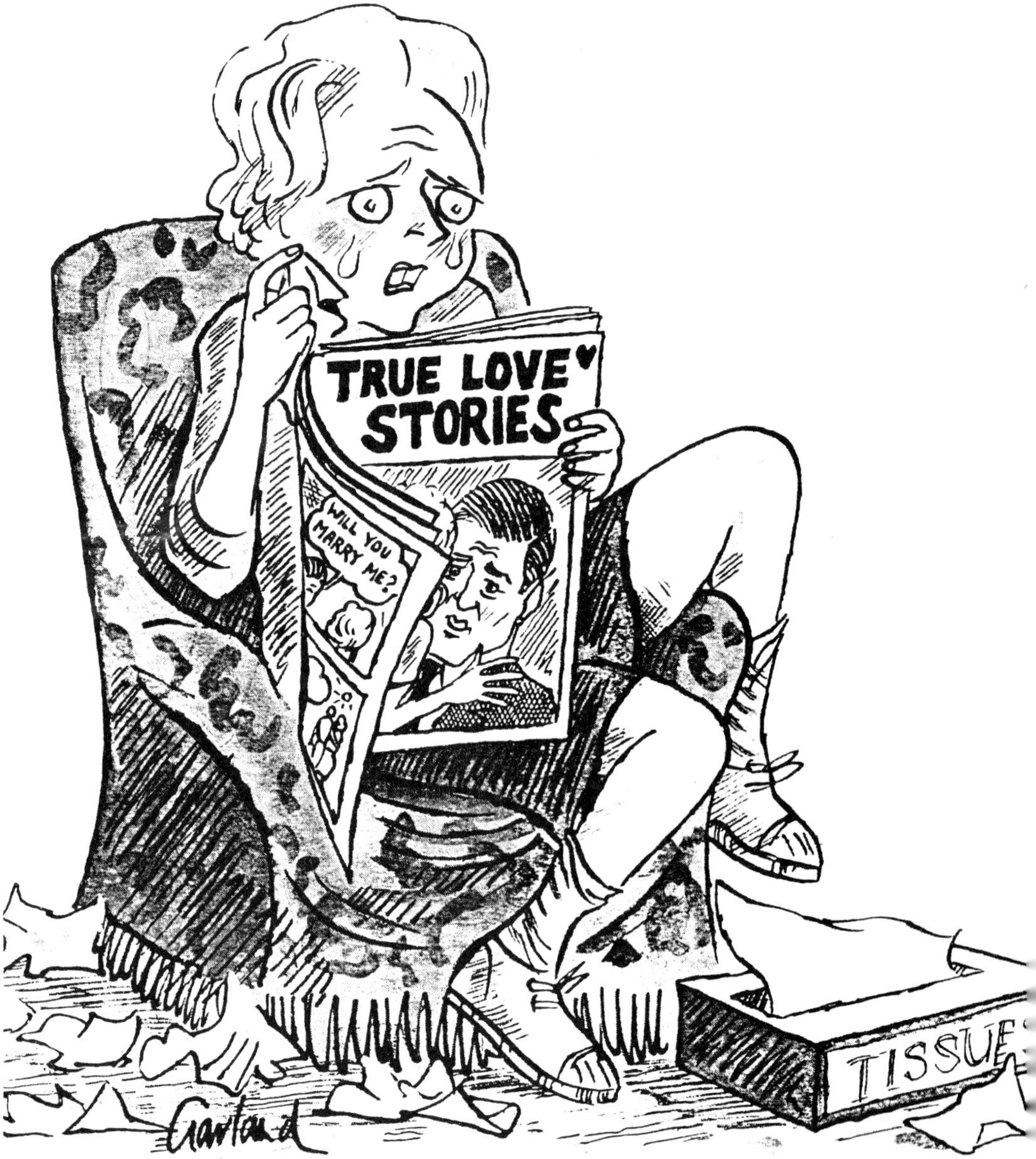
TRUE LOVE STORIES
WILL YOU MARRY ME?
TISSUES
Garland

THE
SPECTATOR
CARTOON BOOK

A Collection of cartoons by
AUSTIN, GARLAND, HEATH
and WOODCOCK.

Introduction by WILLIAM DEEDES

ANDRE DEUTSCH

First published in Great Britain in 1987 by
André Deutsch Limited
105/106 Great Russell Street, London WC1

© 1987 The Spectator

British Library Cataloguing in Publication Data

The Spectator Cartoon Book.
1. English wit and humour, Pictorial
741.5'942   NC1476

ISBN 0 233 98161 6 Hardback
ISBN 0 233 98172 1 Paperback

Printed in Great Britain by
Ebenezer Baylis, Worcester

CONTENTS

INTRODUCTION

We have been slower than the Americans to recognise that the comic artist, if he knows his job, is an extension of editorial comment. I distinguish him from the political cartoonist like Bernard Partridge of long ago, David Low, Vicky and Garland of today. "The Cartoonist" is employed as a political commentator, and in his field we have always had a comfortable edge over the Americans.

Where they have scored is on the comic strip. This was brought home to me some years ago when I rashly determined to procure for the newspaper I was editing a strip cartoon. It was heavy going and ended in total failure. In vain I pointed out that the *Herald Tribune,* perhaps the least racy paper to appear on our bookstands, carried about three-quarters of a page of strips. That, I was told quite wrongly, is because the Americans have simple minds. On the contrary, in this department the Americans are sharper than any of us in Europe. They like their martinis and their humour very dry indeed.

Nevertheless we are coming along. We have no strip cartoon artist comparable to Trudeau who does Doonesbury; but we have developed an art form of our own - the pocket cartoon. No London newspaper, not even those in the A and B readership bracket, scorn a pocket cartoonist on the front page.

Unquestionably the pioneer was Osbert Lancaster, who for a great many years made it perfectly respectable to be seen with a copy of the *Daily Express* in any company. Before some smart Alec writes to tell me that he was not in fact the first pocket cartoonist, let me assert that Maudy Littlehampton was the first woman in any cartoon to make us turn our heads and take a second look, whether we met her in the park, in the street or at the opera.

Both of them have another dimension which has to be approached on tiptoe because it so closely touches class and class consciousness. There has been a long tradition among cartoonists that toffs are always fair game for satirical comment but the lower orders are not. The workers, however, are not immune from Adam's legacy and if we look through Heath's collection, we perceive that he is aware of that. He is every bit as rough on the gormless punk rocker as he is on the foxhunting man.

They will not resent my saying that the best of their work illustrates that all humour in this vein has to be drawn from the same well. One of the cartoons that made me laugh aloud – and other people in the train stare at me rather fixedly – is Heath's joke on page 26, in which the invalid has a large and quite unaccountable vulture sitting on the end of his bed. That drew my mind back to Thurber's lovely drawing of the couple in bed, with one observing to the other: "I thought I heard a seal bark!" A large seal is peering over the back of the bed behind them.

A lot of pocket cartoons, even in a weekly like the *Spectator,* are too closely related to current events to qualify for a volume like this. But observe how many have survived the test of time. What the best of writers and the best of cartoonists achieve in very small company is clear insight into the nature of man, which (alas) changes very little indeed.

Evelyn Waugh had this gift of insight, which is why his books date very little. At one time, under Ross, the *New Yorker's* cartoonists like Peter Arno had the gift. The best of Heath and the best of Austin on these pages possess it. Why not? The human comedy is played on a revolving stage.

What is that you are shouting at me from the back of the hall? Jane? Oh, Jane of the *Mirror?* Point taken, but Jane was in every sense of the word a strip, and we are discussing pocket cartoons.

At his best, and in the collection which the *Spectator* has put together we encounter some of the best, the pocket cartoonist is not simply an extension of editorial comment but an indispensable addition to it. He is indispensable because he can convey with a couple of figures and a short caption a message which would be infernally hard, perhaps impossible, to convey in an editorial comment.

Cast your eye over the tiny cartoon by Heath on page 46. Husband and wife furiously confront each other over the breakfast table. "You say there's nothing in the paper; I say there's a whole forest." That is a sharper comment on Greens who suffer from an excess of zeal than any editorial writer could contrive. Look again at Austin's tiny drawing in the Love and Sex section of a woman staring at signposts marked Marriage and Love. As the old *News of the World* would have said, all human life is there.

A thought has occured to me looking over this collection. I get a feeling that, with the notable exception of my colleague Peter Simple, the sharpest comment on the human comedy – which we call satire – has shifted from writers to artists. We are not over endowed just now with people who can produce verse like Chesterton', quips like Coward's or prose like Muggeridge's. Perhaps that is because nobody today seems to have time to read anything. Even to the most slow-witted among us, Heath and Austin can get their message across in something under five seconds.

WILLIAM DEEDES

POLITICS
AND
POWER

Descent of Tory Man

'PR-wise, "bridge-building" is the wrong image.'

'Oh Dave, can't we forget about acid rain just for Christmas?'

'What was the English Channel, Daddy?'

'Welcome to these informal discussions, gentleman.'

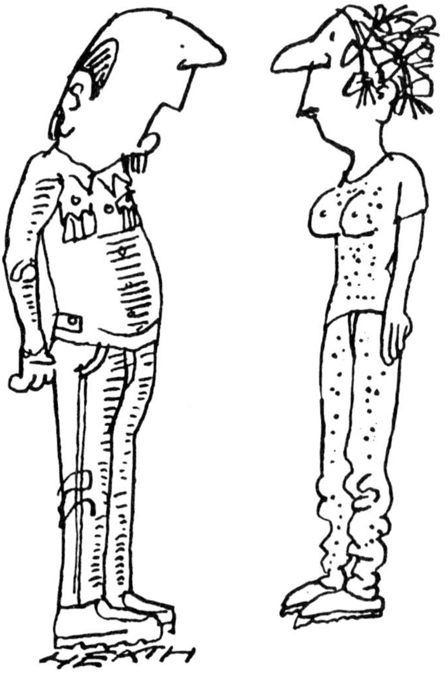
HEATH

'People who want to bring back hanging
should be shot.'

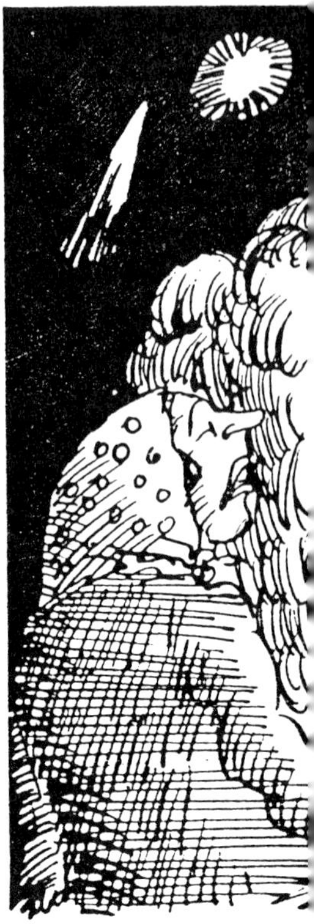

'He failed to blow u
year he's

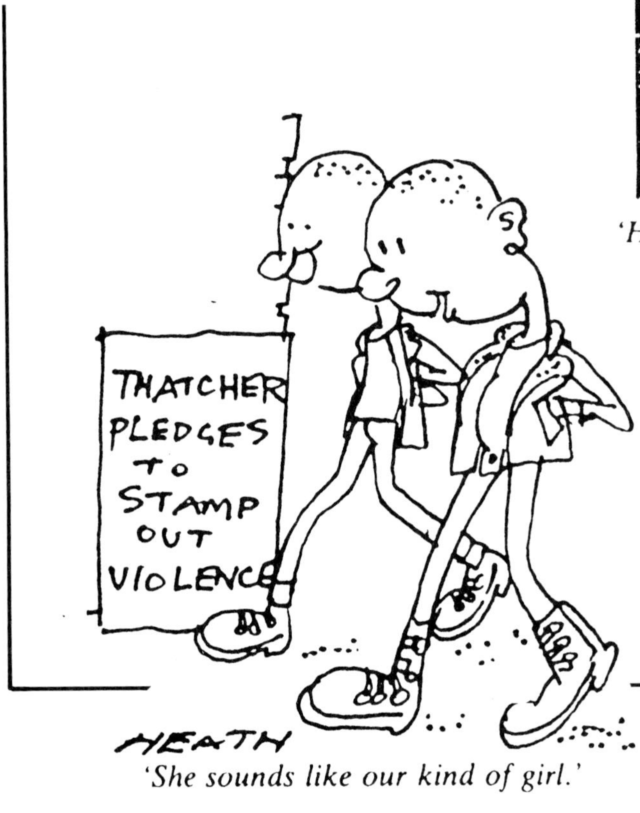
THATCHER
PLEDGES
TO
STAMP
OUT
VIOLENCE
HEATH

'She sounds like our kind of girl.'

...arliament, so every ...urned in effigy.'

'You chaps told me you were freemasons.'

'It must be nice for him to know that some-
one was listening to him.'

'You must take mid-term unpopularity into account.'

'Our president may be old, but at least he's not dead.'

'Put me down as unskilled — I was an MP.'

'KGB card — that'll do nicely, sir.'

'I expect he listens to his own speeches.'

'Put another peace plan on the fire. It's getting cold'.

'It's not fair. You've had the gun all morning.'

'Maybe another twenty years of speech therapy and I'll be ready to run for President.'

'I won't be long, I'm just going for a leak.'

'I suppose you could put it down to race prejudice.'

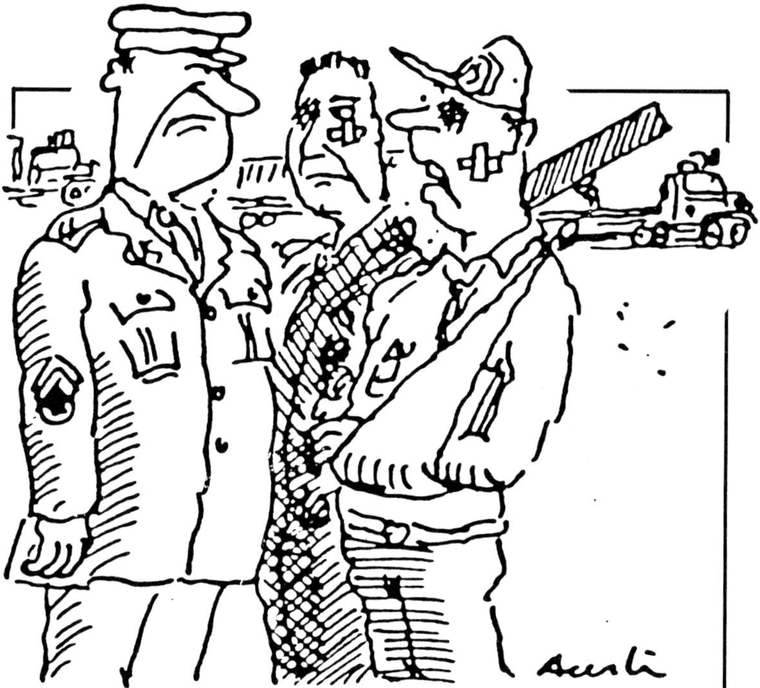

'We ran into some peace people.'

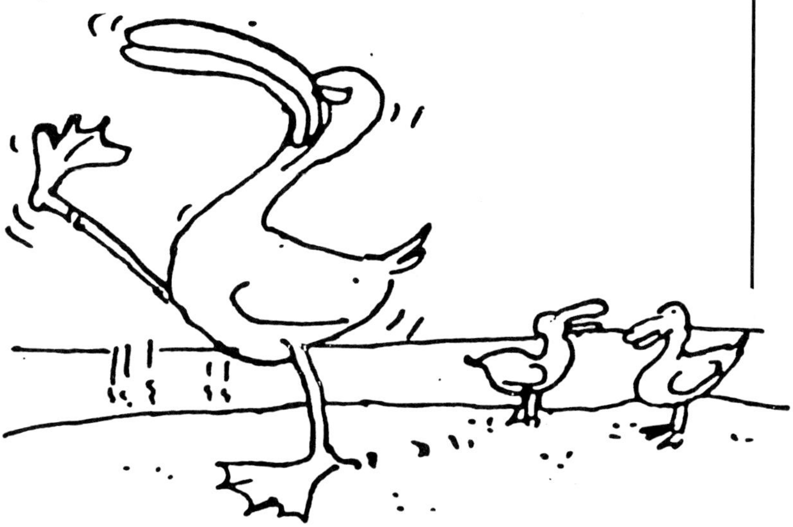

'He's been a militarist since his ancestors took territory from Lorenz.'

FOOD, DRINK AND HEALTH

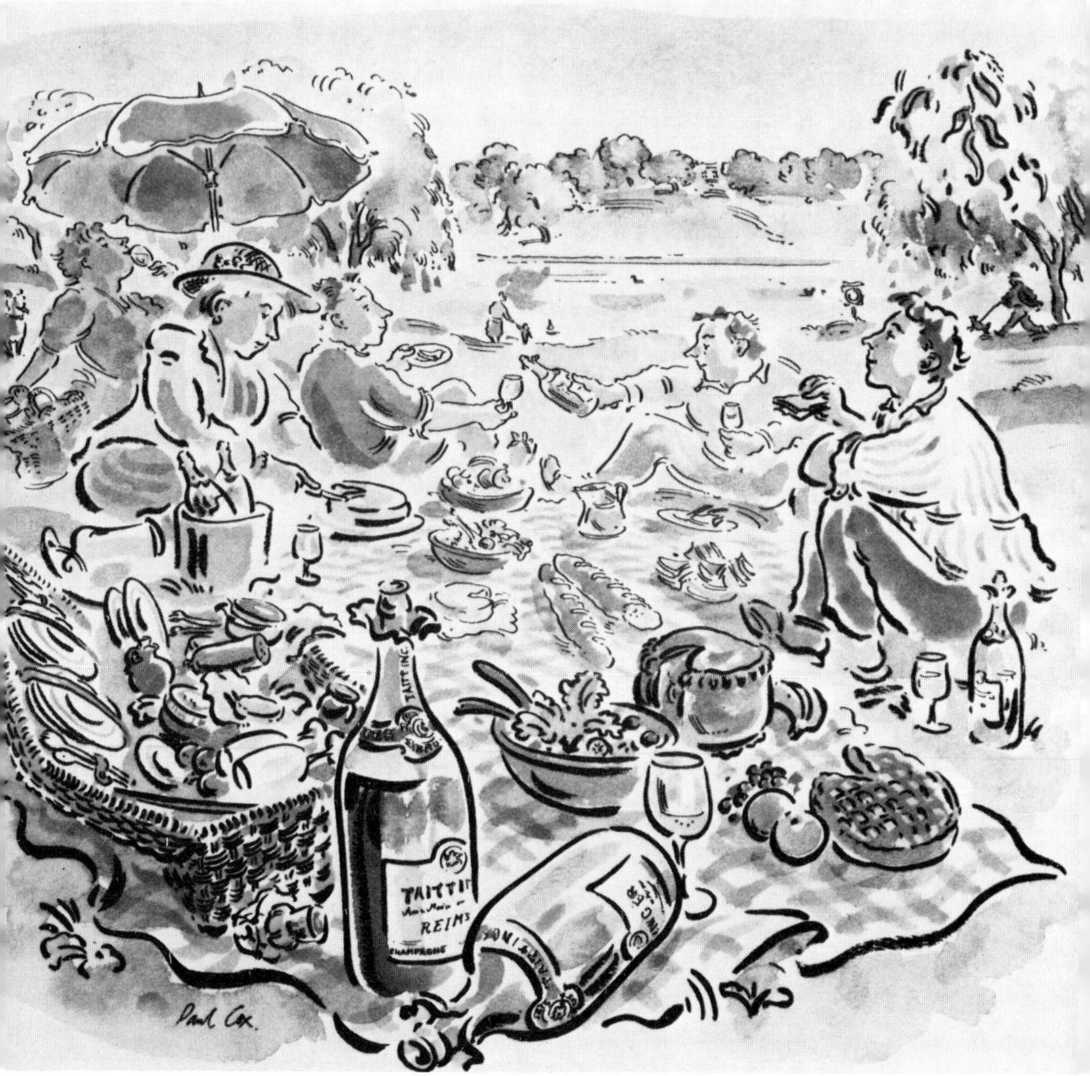
REIMS

'I see your baboon transplant works, Dr. Moreau.'

'Is there a second opinion in the house?'

'I felt so guilty about smoking and drinking
I took to drugs.'

'I'm so depressed th

'It's the only advertisement for tobacco that
the BMA will accept.'

'It looks like he's tak

'maritans ring me.'

'Have you got any organic glue?'

urn for the worse.'

'Since we rescued him from an experimental laboratory we've got him down to ten a day.'

'I don't make house calls. I failed the bedside manner examination.'

'If your mind's really made up, take this kidney donor card.'

'I'm trying to refute wine snob.

'Can you afford to keep my daughter in the drug habit she's accustomed to?'

'Of course you're sick, I

...gation that I'm a

'Dickon — it's a plagueogram.'

...son, the whole world is sick.'

'There's a strong aftertaste of hype.'

'I heard you're a genius — why is it you're not drunk?'

'They're fitness fanatics, demanding that we stop drinking and eat muesli.'

'Don't worry. It's not a hold-up, I'm just a secret drinker.'

'Thanks for your help, officer, but I'm not protesting, I'm just pissed.'

'Darling, I'm going to be a surrogate mother.'

'Monsieur wants a second helping?'

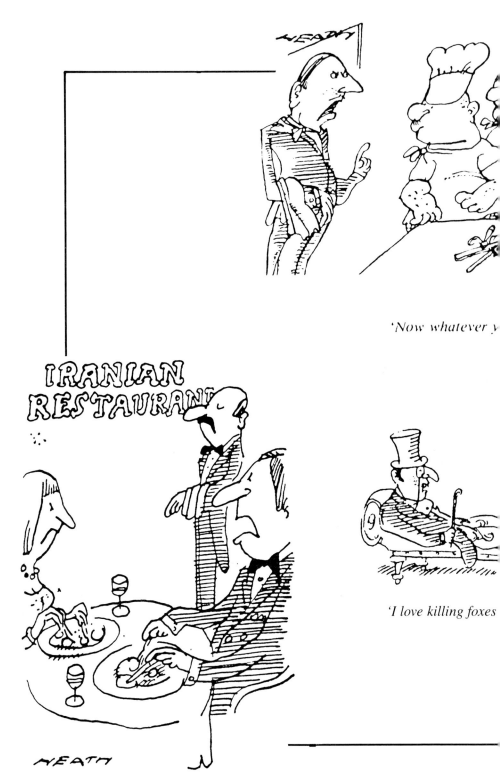

'Now whatever y

'I love killing foxes

'Now I know why they go on hunger strike!'

'...don't spoil it!'

HEATH

'Now eat it all up! There are thousands of
Western children forced to be on a diet!'

'My compliments to the chef.'

'He drinks too much'

'Mind if I passive smoke?'

'It's the unhappy hour, sir — all drinks are
ten pence extra.'

'Were you complaining about the broth?'

'The trouble is, I can never get fit enough to use the equipment'.

'They call me waiter, but you've been waiting for half an hour.'

ARTS AND THE MEDIA

The Fight for Quality

'It's Prince Charles offering us pictures of our photographers.'

'It's nice to see a
people ha

'She's been a right pain ever since s

STALLS
←

*ort where only two
·ach other.'

'I liked the show too, so what on earth are
we going to write about it?'

's filmed by David Attenborough.'

NEWS
WIMBLEDON
LATEST

NEATH

NEATH

'It's a gossip column.'

'Those of you who would like Haml[...]'

'God knows what we're going to show you today, but you'll watch anything, so what the hell.'

'ry Ophelia and settle down, vote now.'

'We demand an end to the media stereotyp-
ing of gays.'

47

'Surely it's not that bad a newspaper.'

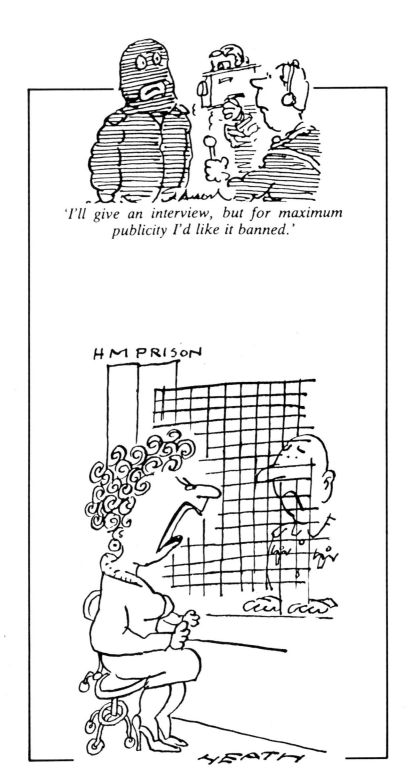

'I'll give an interview, but for maximum
publicity I'd like it banned.'

'Trust you to commit a crime that was of no
interest to a journalist with a cheque book.'

'Oh, it's just a little book I've written.'

'It may see

'I had my hair done by Henry Moore.'

'You say there's nothir
there's a wh

50

HEATH

'... pensive, but I had to have a plumber to instal it.'

'... the paper; I say ...rest.'

'That's a pity, I was hoping to see nipples and Di.'

NEWS
ROYAL
WEDDING
T SHIRTS
BANNED

'Take me to your leader writer.'

'My novel came in at seven pounds three
ounces and is doing very well.'

'It's not in the catalogue, mister, it's my push-chair.'

'It's a sex-objet d'art.'

'We'll get nowhere without a video.'

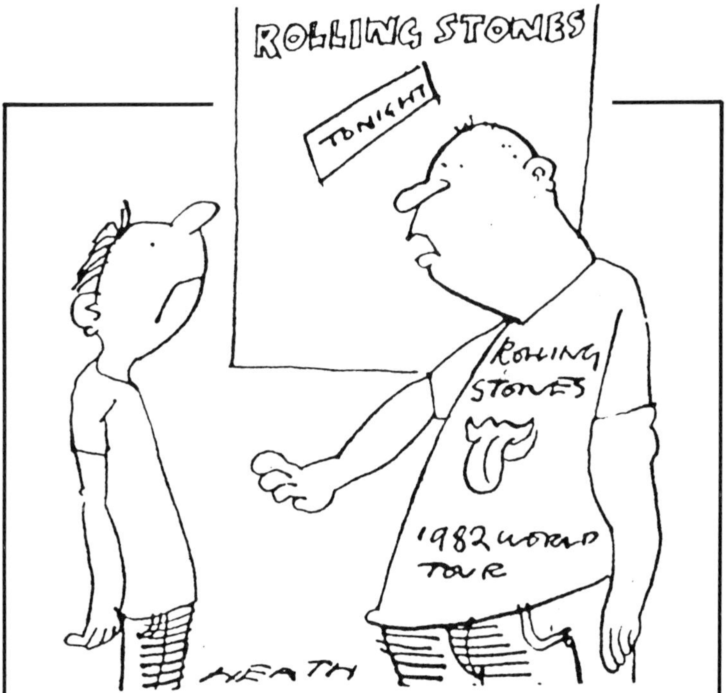
ROLLING STONES
TONIGHT
ROLLING
STONES
1982 WORLD
TOUR
HEATH

'Sorry, son, you can't come in — you're under 40.'

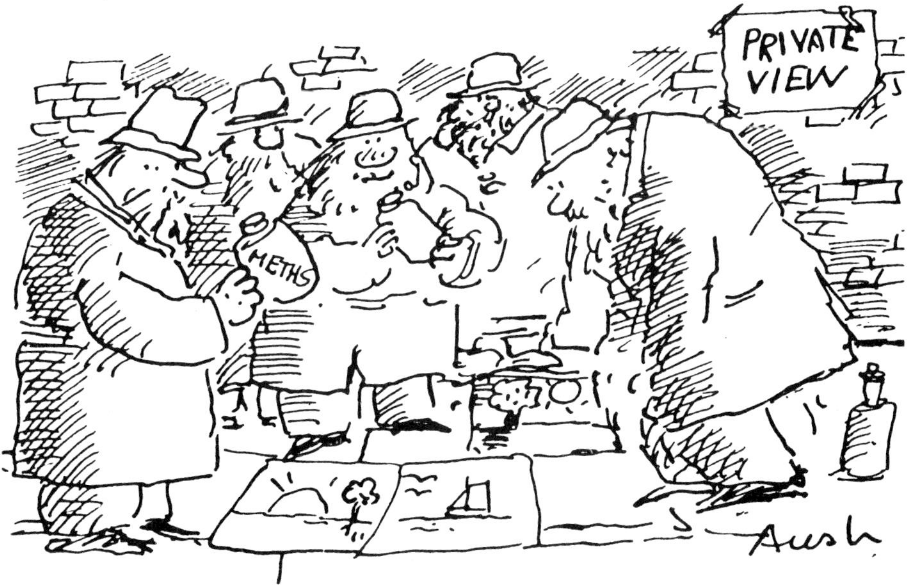
PRIVATE
VIEW
METHS
Aush

'It's a mystery. One of the most successful art collectors in the world and he goes and hangs himself.'

'Come in, I'm watching a video-nice.'

'It's how I see a phallic symbol.'

SEX AND MARRIAGE

Part-time Lovers

'I don't know

'Call me an old stick-in-the-mud, but I still like women.'

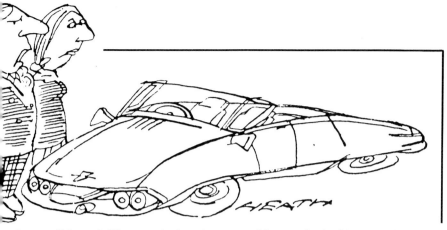

...they call it a virility symbol — it got to 90 m.p.h. in 30 seconds and then conked out.'

HOLLYWOOD
BLOW-A-KISS-FROM
A-SAFE-DISTANCE-
O-GRAM

'This is Sylvia, my grumbling appendix.'

I suggest a thirty year trial separation.

'The sanctity of shacking up together
means nothing to you?'

'I'm going back to your mother.'

'I'm English — and if I come out of anything I'll come out of a cupboard.'

IF THEY TRY TO SUE YOU I'M SUE TRY ME

SOLICITORS

'My other inflatable
doesn't understand ͏'

'You've got a lot to learn about the art of begging.'

'You never speak to me now that you have a w

'You've been jogging with another woman.'

'Even buying h

'Thank you Mr Smith — without my glasses you're tolerably attractive too.'

EATH

essor.'

'I hasn't cured his tendency to adopt a stereotyped sex role.'

'I wish to make it quite clear Mr Hotchkiss, that I am not a sexual object.'

'And just where do you think you are taking me, Miss Simpkins?'

'Look, I hope you don't mind, but your mother and I got married today.'

'This is going to put the magic back into our marriage.'

And it was in this building that Dickens is supposed to have got the idea for 'Little Dorrit'.

'Give it to me straight! There's another test-tube isn't there!'

'Fancy a professional foul?'

'Adultery is now OK, and I'm also loving
my neighbour.'

'Whatever happened to repenting at leisure?'

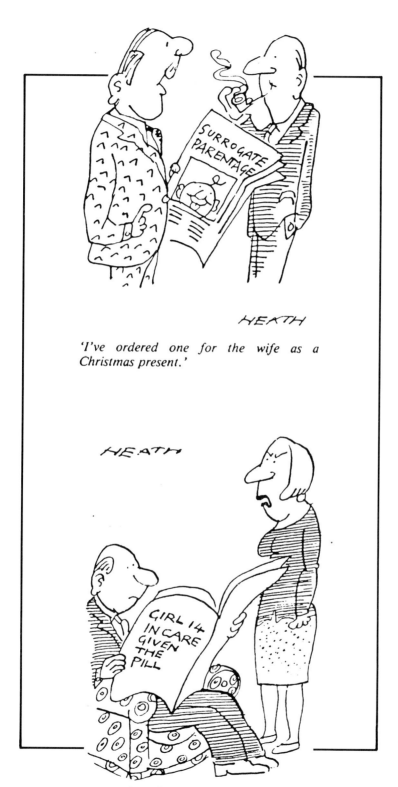

HEATH

'I've ordered one for the wife as a Christmas present.'

HEATH

'In my day all we had were gobstoppers.'

MODERN
LIVING

The New Young Rich

'Of course, the school fees are rather high, so our son Rodney has to do a bit of mugging to help out.'

'I'd like figure.'

ANOTHER IDIOT WITH WRITING ON HIS TEE SHIRT

KEVIN WOODCOCK

...in as an establishment

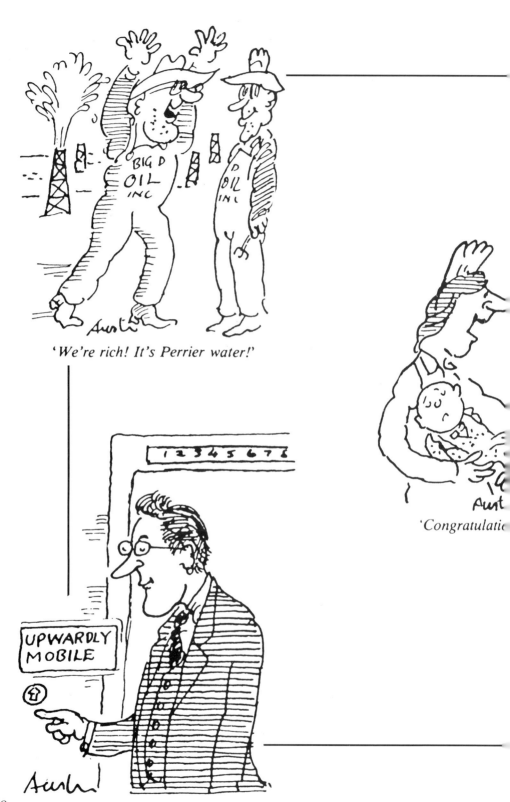

'We're rich! It's Perrier water!'

'Congratulatic

UPWARDLY
MOBILE

'They rather got up my nose, too!'

a fogey.'

'Tragic case — he was with the video squad but became depraved watching the nasty ones.'

'No

'Jim spent so much time there, he decided to go down with it'

'We may be getting there, but you won't.'

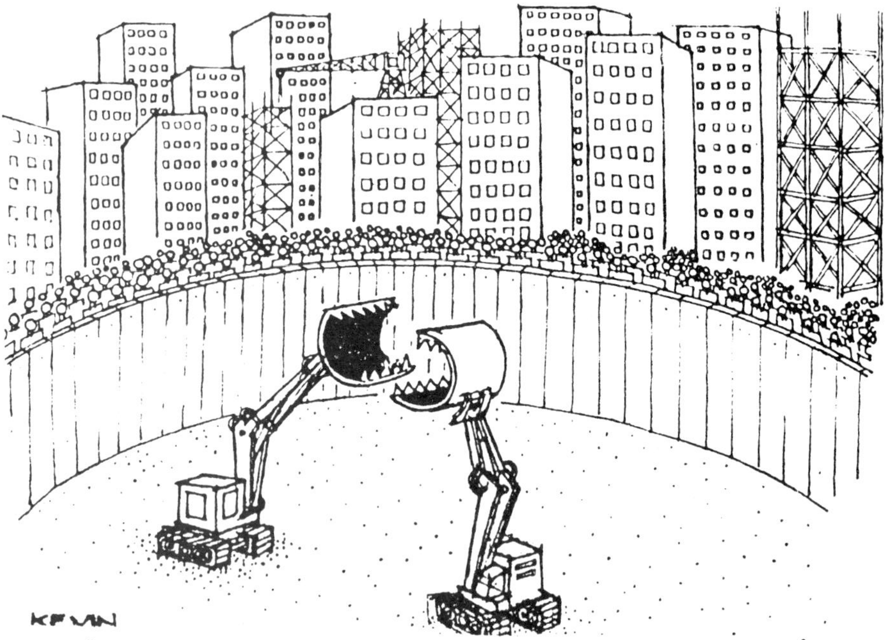

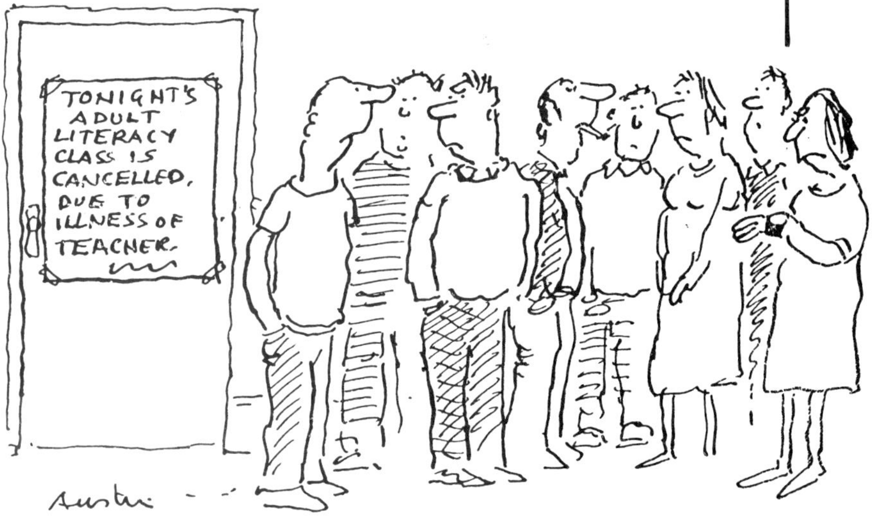
TONIGHT'S ADULT LITERACY CLASS IS CANCELLED, DUE TO ILLNESS OF TEACHER.

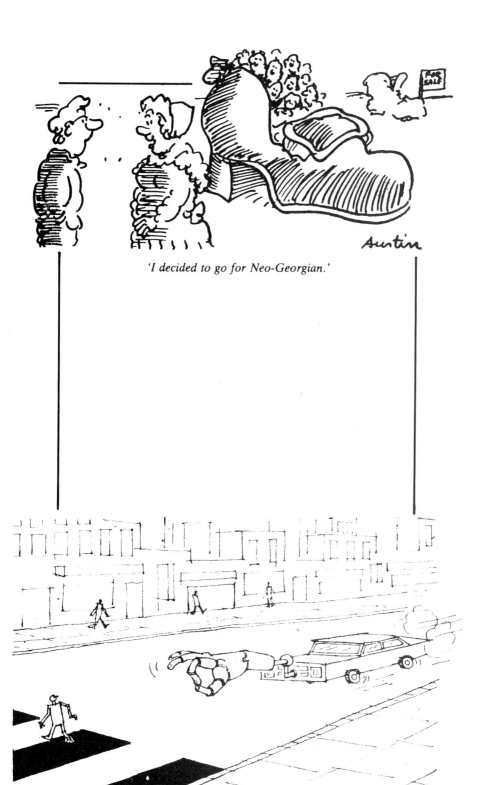

'I decided to go for Neo-Georgian.'

Austin

KEVIN WOODCOCK

HOSPITAL

HEATH

'Your father died two hours ago but don't worry, we've got the whole thing on video.'

'It's an obj

SKIN
DOMIN
REIGN
HOLD SWAY
GOVERN _

THE

Austin

CLUB 1830

's it d'art?'

'Officer, this man's got his hand up my trousers.'

'When your work experience scheme is over
you'll move straight on to our out of work
experience scheme.'

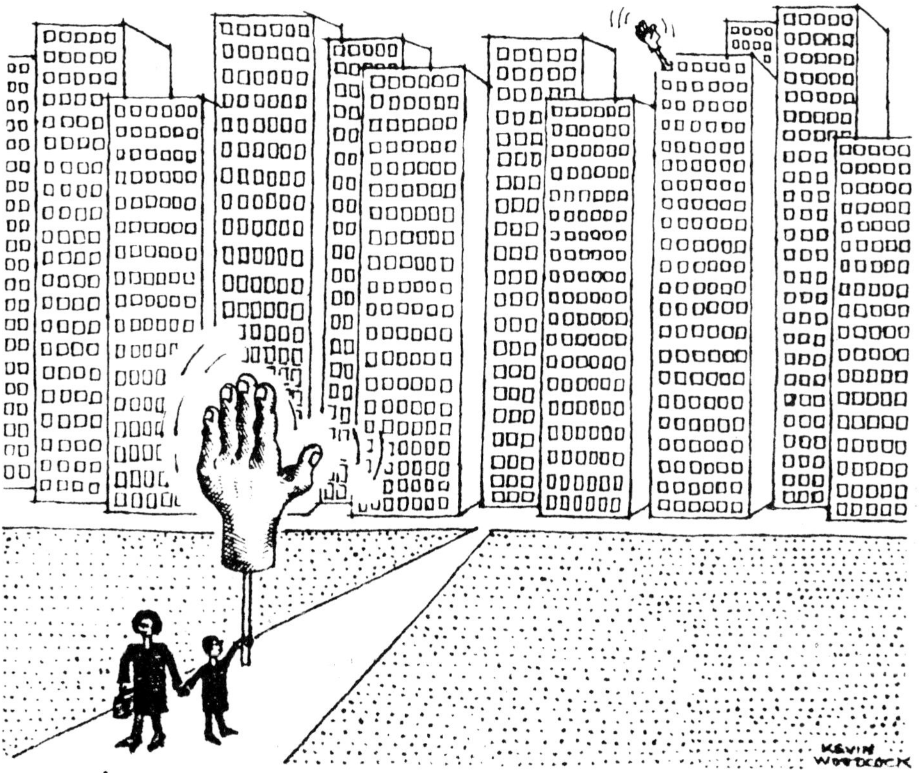
KEVIN WOODCOCK

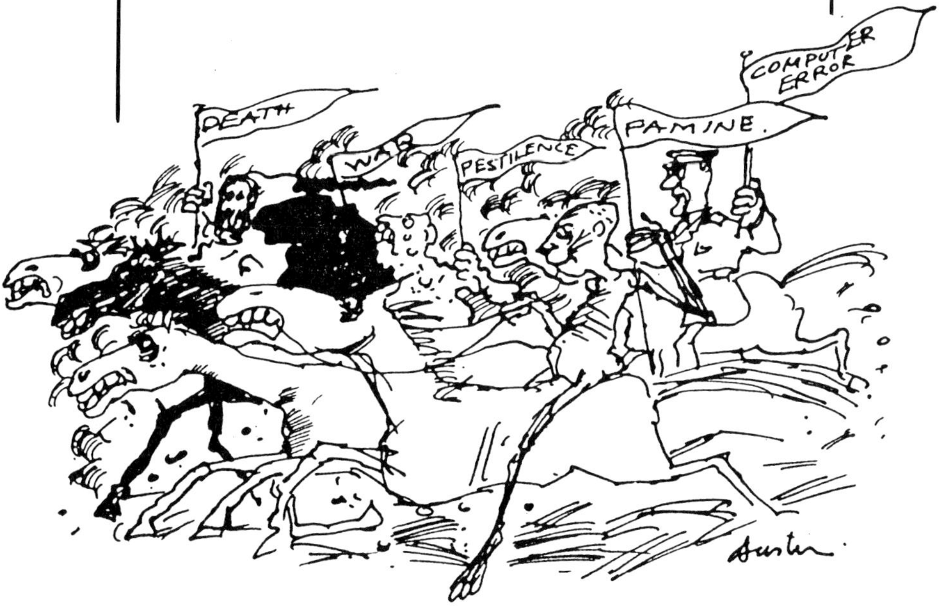
DEATH
WAR
PESTILENCE
FAMINE
COMPUTER ERROR
Austin

'I don't understand it, George and I have bought every consumer durable we're still unhappy.'

'It's a good way to get a carriage to yourself.'

'Rela

'My God! The portrait of Christian Barnard.'

aid that you give 'em a pair of nylons and they'll eat out of your hand.'

RELIGION

The Church Vanishes

'Smoking or non-smoking?'

'To Hell with it! I'm going topless.'

'I've established a religion that really appeals to people.'

'Come on, just for a laugh.'

93

'Sorry, Guv. Office party.'

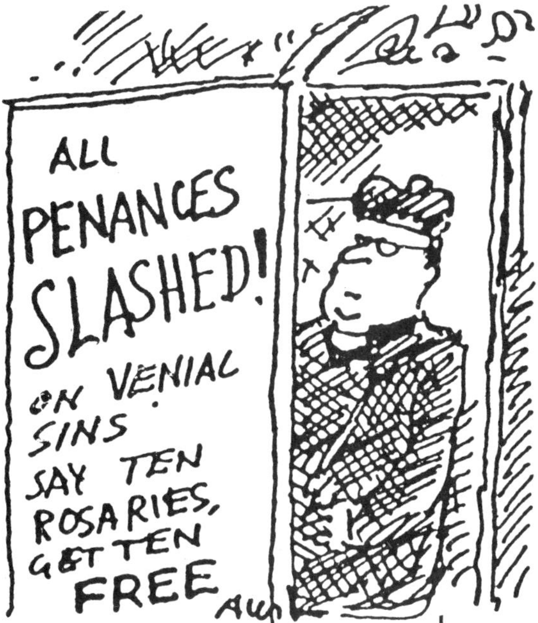
ALL
PENANCES
SLASHED!
ON VENIAL
SINS
SAY TEN
ROSARIES,
GET TEN
FREE

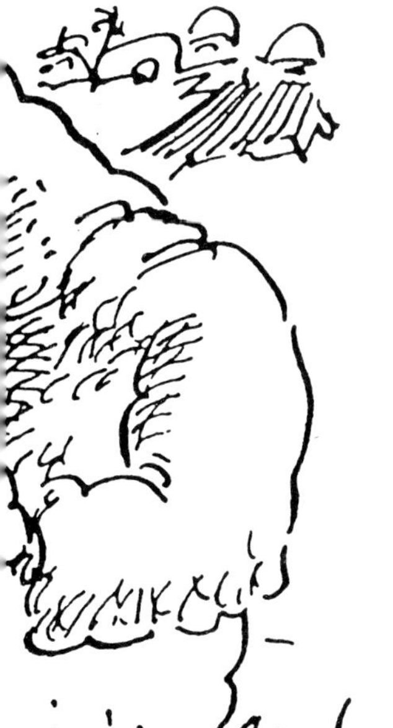

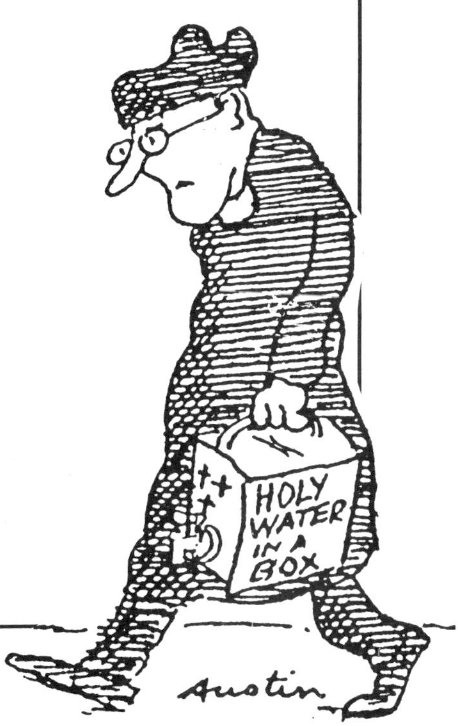
HOLY
WATER
IN A
BOX
Austin

'Well, it will get them into church at least twice in a lifetime.'

'No thanks, I never eat fast food.'

'That was no actress that was my wife!'

BESTIARY

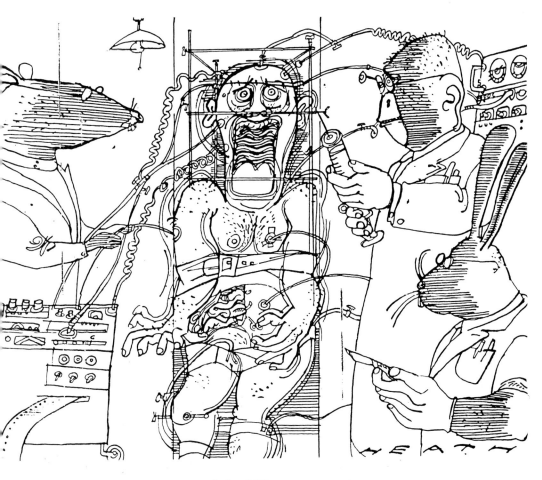

Animal Wrongs

'. . . so the horrid prince turned into a nice, harmless frog.'

'I think we ought to give serious thought to arms limitati

'He's got a gnu.'

'Free range, eh? Prove it!'

101

'I was expecting a wolf.'

'We demand flexible roostering.'

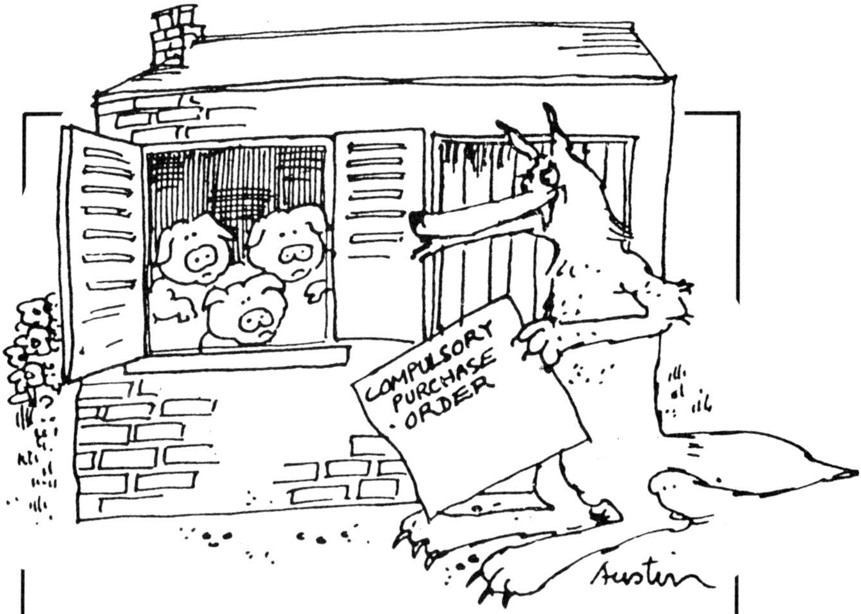
COMPULSORY PURCHASE ORDER

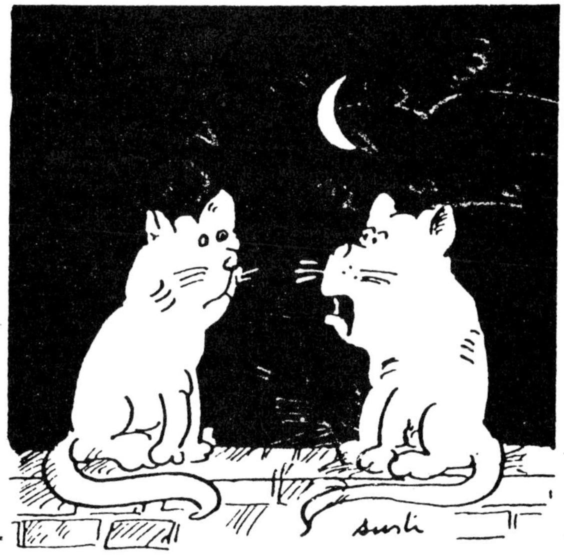

'Sorry, I've been positively vetted.'

'The way I see it we lost Bo Peep.'

'Damr

'That's what I call a guide dog.'

'Full moon — that means six months' quarantine.'

'You swear it's not South African?'

HEATH

'I feel so sorry for them pacing up and down like that.'

'We gave up using animals because we thought it was too cruel.'

'I used to watch the feathered variety but it was so boring.'

'I'm at a loss for a simile to describe the way we breed.'

'What's the matter with you? You're not very jumpy today.'

'Constable Jones is our decoy.'

'Ignore it. It's the silly season.'

'I think all the money from the book spoiled Peter.'

'A grand on the tortoise to win.'

'Have you ever wondered why we're
aerodynamically styled?'

'I'm streetwise.'

'I'm insider dealing.'

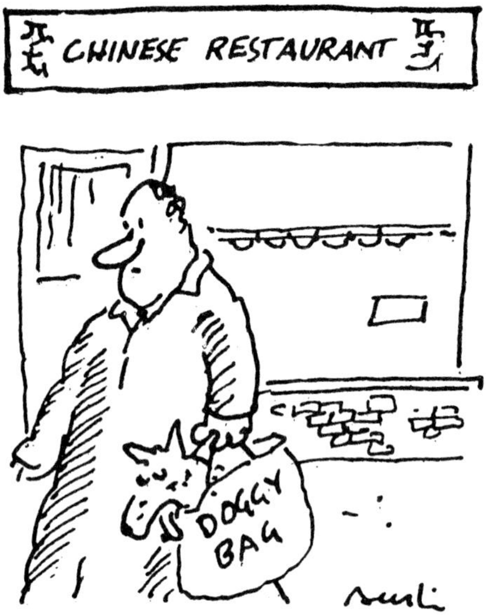
CHINESE RESTAURANT
DOGGY BAG

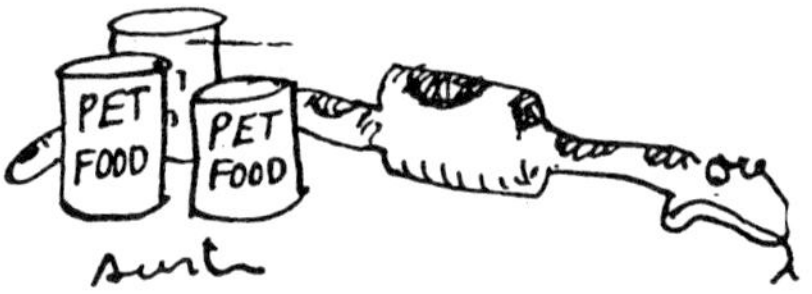
PET FOOD
PET FOOD

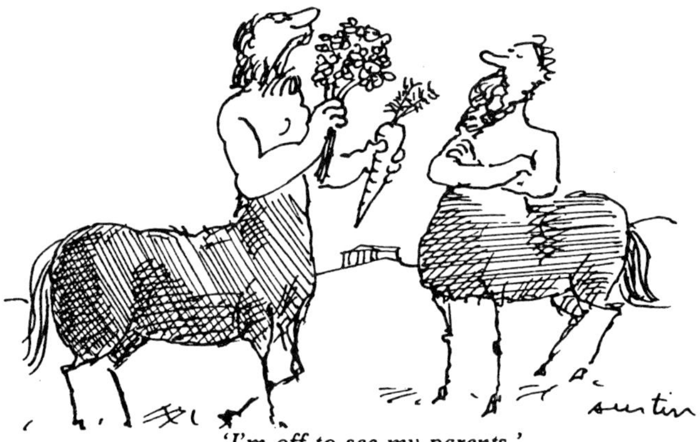

'I'm off to see my parents.'